PROTESTING FOR CHANGE

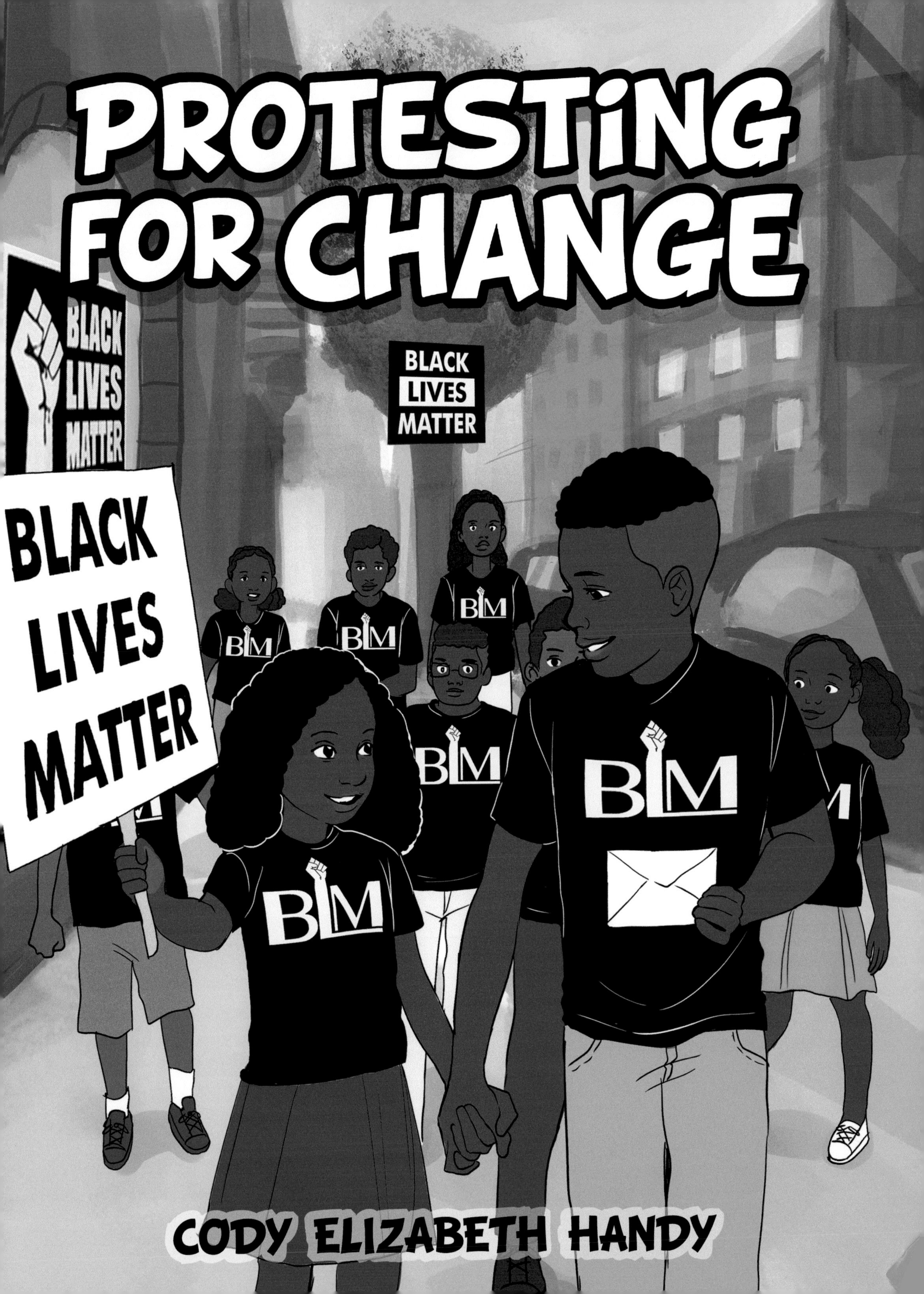

CODY ELIZABETH HANDY

To order additional copies of this book, contact:
Xlibris
844-714-8691
www.Xlibris.com
Orders@Xlibris.com

ISBN: Softcover   978-1-6698-1132-9
        EBook   978-1-6698-1131-2

Print information available on the last page

Rev. date: 02/21/2022

PROTESTING FOR CHANGE

CODY ELIZABETH HANDY

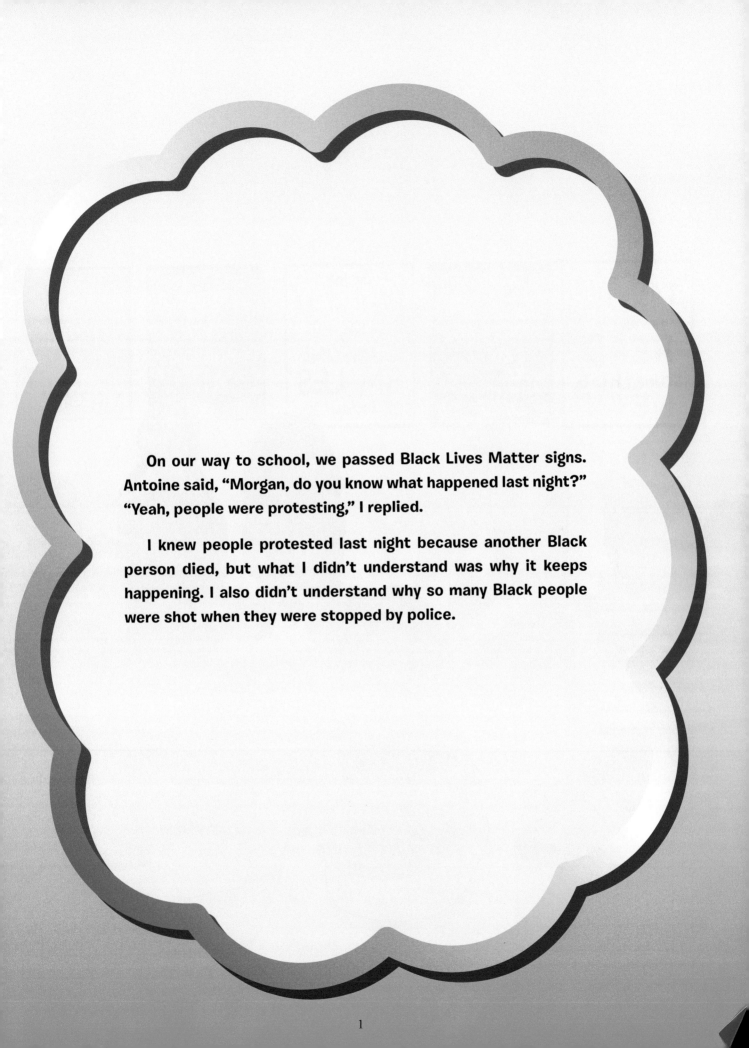

On our way to school, we passed Black Lives Matter signs. Antoine said, "Morgan, do you know what happened last night?" "Yeah, people were protesting," I replied.

I knew people protested last night because another Black person died, but what I didn't understand was why it keeps happening. I also didn't understand why so many Black people were shot when they were stopped by police.

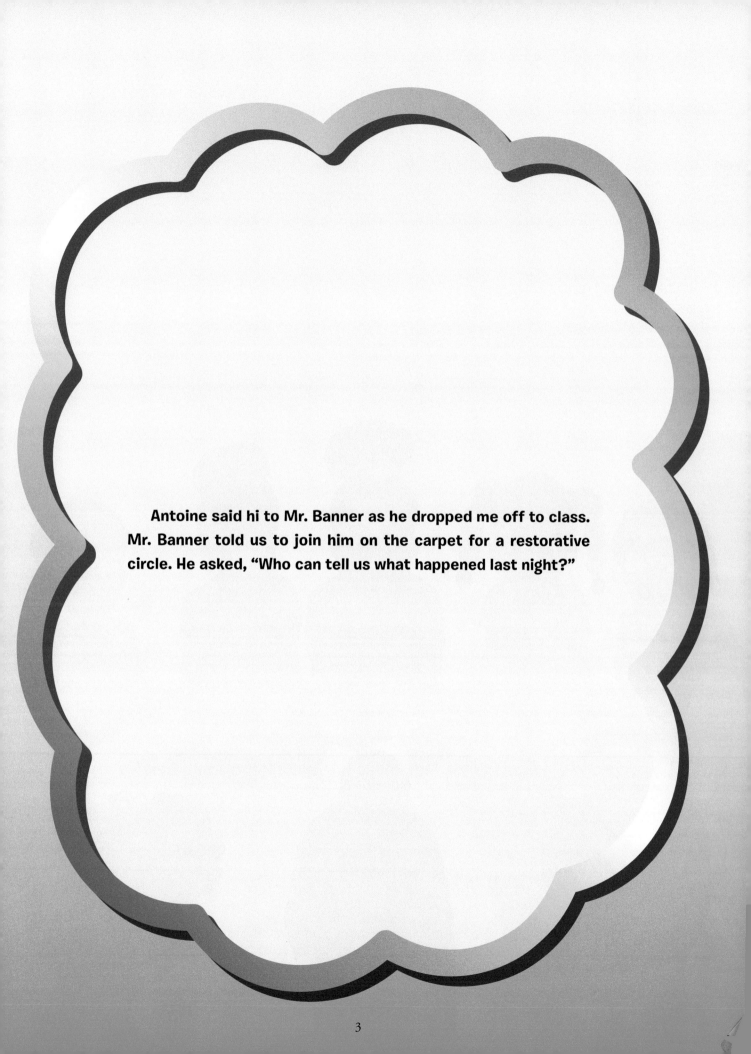

Antoine said hi to Mr. Banner as he dropped me off to class. Mr. Banner told us to join him on the carpet for a restorative circle. He asked, "Who can tell us what happened last night?"

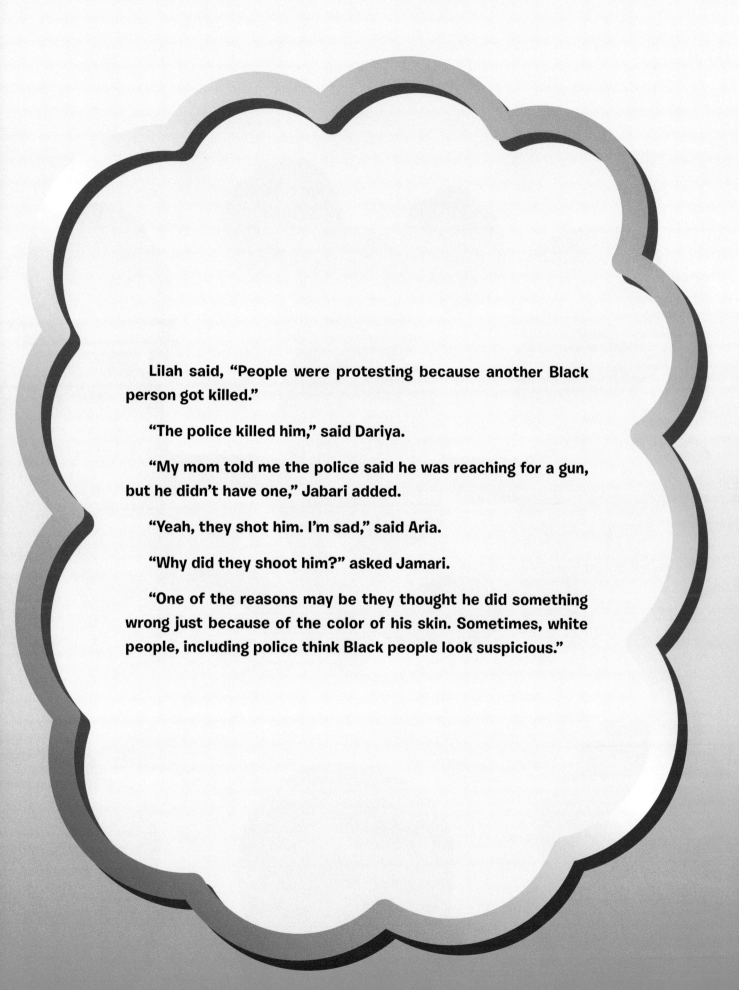

Lilah said, "People were protesting because another Black person got killed."

"The police killed him," said Dariya.

"My mom told me the police said he was reaching for a gun, but he didn't have one," Jabari added.

"Yeah, they shot him. I'm sad," said Aria.

"Why did they shoot him?" asked Jamari.

"One of the reasons may be they thought he did something wrong just because of the color of his skin. Sometimes, white people, including police think Black people look suspicious."

Ava said, "That's wrong. Just because someone is Black, people shouldn't think they did something bad."

"It's not fair," responded Jarell.

"You're right. It's not fair and that is why people were protesting," said Mr. Banner.

"I still don't understand why they shot him," responded Jamari.

"A lot of people don't, Jamari," said Mr. Banner. "That is why a lot of people are angry and sad. It's the reason they are demanding answers and change."

Mr. Banner continued, "Some police feel they can use their power against them. Police use this force against Black people more than they do on white people. Not all police, but some. This is called police brutality. People are protesting to end this."

"How do you think the people who were protesting are feeling and why?" Mr. Banner asked.

"I think they were angry because the police killed another Black person," Louisa said.

Nori added, "I think they were mad because it's not okay. It shouldn't have happened."

"I think some might have been sad because it keeps happening," said Xavier.

"Maybe they were frustrated because nothing is changing," said Davia.

"My dad said police shot a Black person before, and he was walking away," Karter added.

"My mom always told me that when someone does something bad, they go to jail. But when police kill a Black person they don't. I don't understand. It makes me mad." Ciarra stated.

Mr. Banner said, "It is upsetting to hear and see these things happen. Black people being treated differently based on the color of their skin and killed for it, is racism. Black people being pulled over four to five times more than white people is racism. It is unfair, and needs to change. That is why people are protesting. They are demanding change."

Mr. Banner said, "Let's talk about what you saw and heard during the protests last night."

"I saw people carrying signs," chimed in Chrissette.

"What did the signs say?" Mr. Banner asked.

"Black Lives Matter." "I Can't Breathe." "Say Their Names." "Enough!" "Justice Brings Peace." "End Police Brutality."

"I saw lots of people marching, and heard them chanting 'Black Lives Matter,'" said Darnell.

"I also heard them chanting, 'No Justice. No Peace,'" added Kyon.

Mr. Banner said, "Those signs and words were the message of the protest."

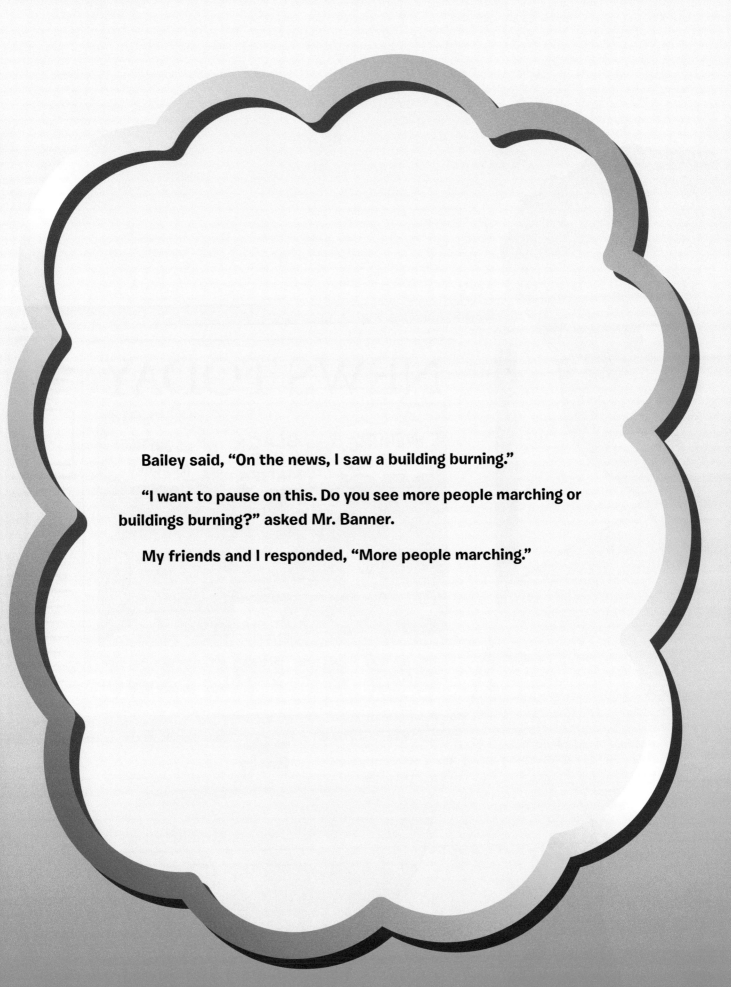

Bailey said, "On the news, I saw a building burning."

"I want to pause on this. Do you see more people marching or buildings burning?" asked Mr. Banner.

My friends and I responded, "More people marching."

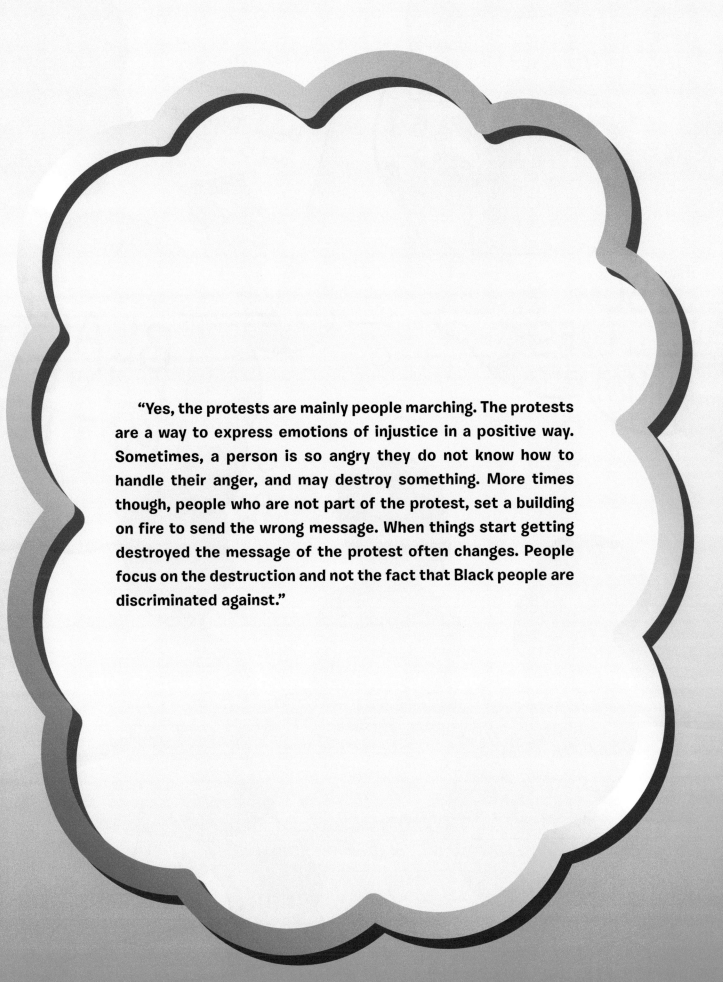

"Yes, the protests are mainly people marching. The protests are a way to express emotions of injustice in a positive way. Sometimes, a person is so angry they do not know how to handle their anger, and may destroy something. More times though, people who are not part of the protest, set a building on fire to send the wrong message. When things start getting destroyed the message of the protest often changes. People focus on the destruction and not the fact that Black people are discriminated against."

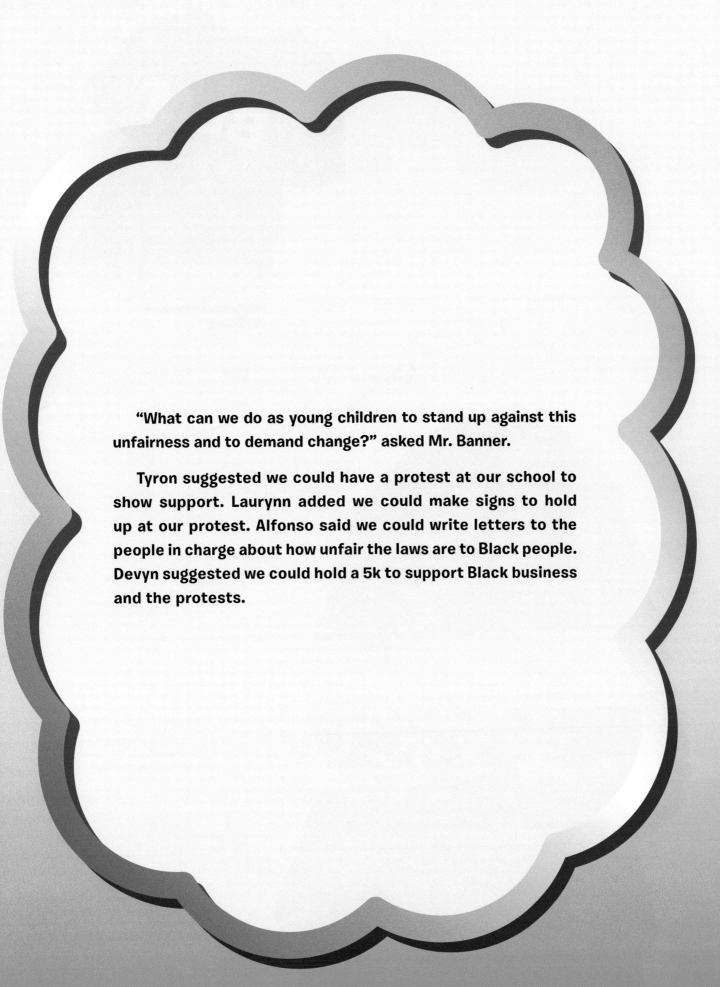

"What can we do as young children to stand up against this unfairness and to demand change?" asked Mr. Banner.

Tyron suggested we could have a protest at our school to show support. Laurynn added we could make signs to hold up at our protest. Alfonso said we could write letters to the people in charge about how unfair the laws are to Black people. Devyn suggested we could hold a 5k to support Black business and the protests.

I said, "We could wear our Black Lives Matter shirts to show support." The class liked the idea. We decided we would all wear them to school tomorrow. We also decided to make signs to bring to school. Mr. Banner said he would work on the protest, and we would write letters another day.

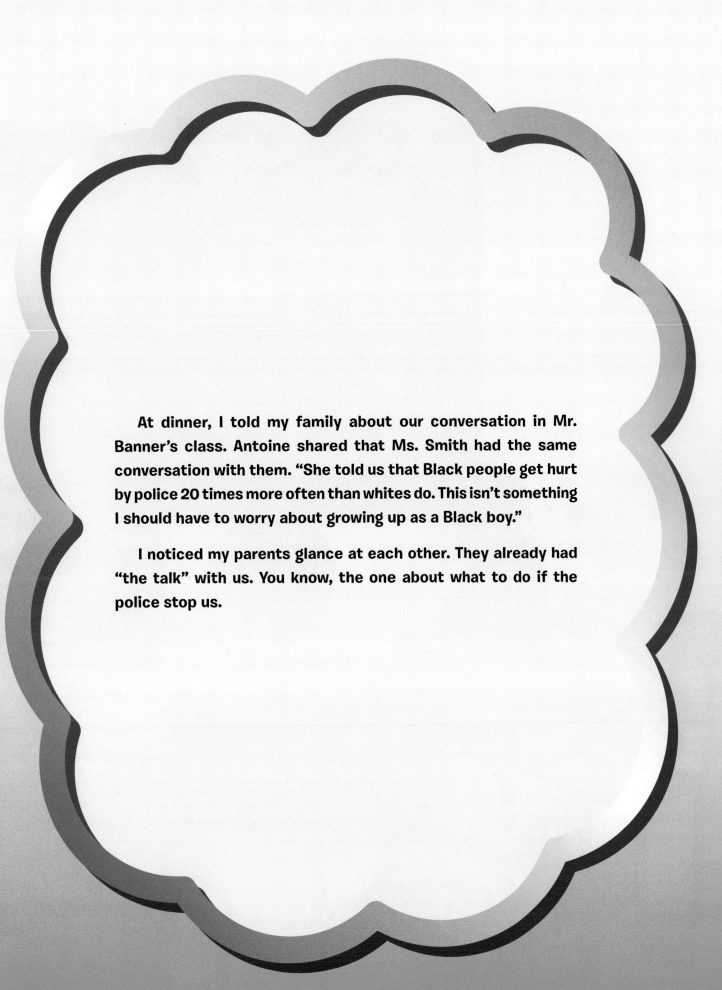

At dinner, I told my family about our conversation in Mr. Banner's class. Antoine shared that Ms. Smith had the same conversation with them. "She told us that Black people get hurt by police 20 times more often than whites do. This isn't something I should have to worry about growing up as a Black boy."

I noticed my parents glance at each other. They already had "the talk" with us. You know, the one about what to do if the police stop us.

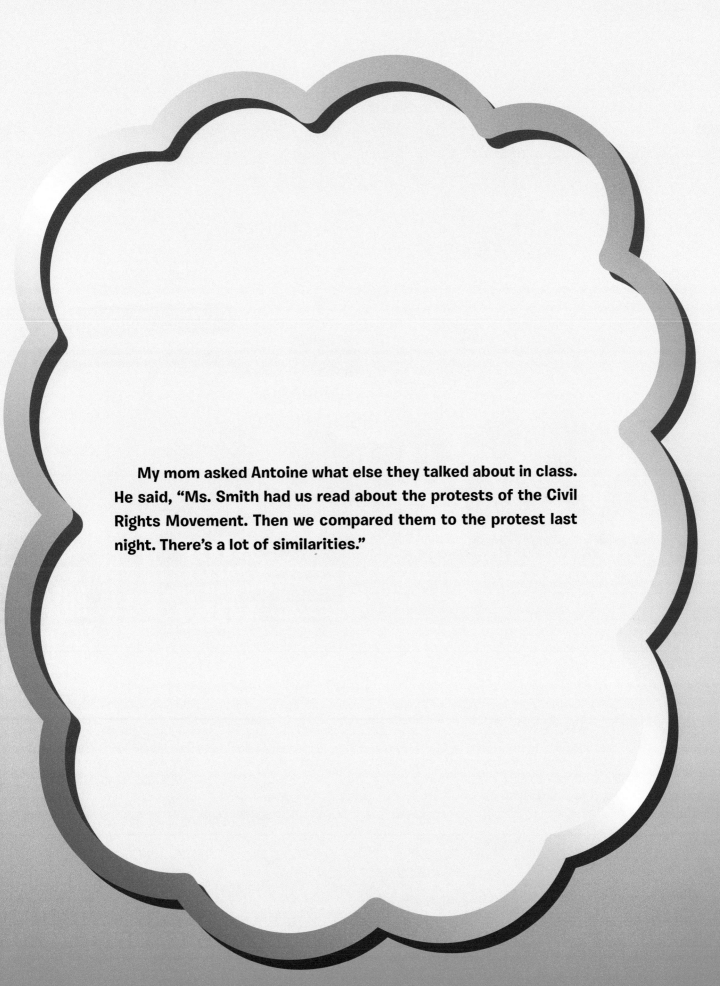

My mom asked Antoine what else they talked about in class. He said, "Ms. Smith had us read about the protests of the Civil Rights Movement. Then we compared them to the protest last night. There's a lot of similarities."

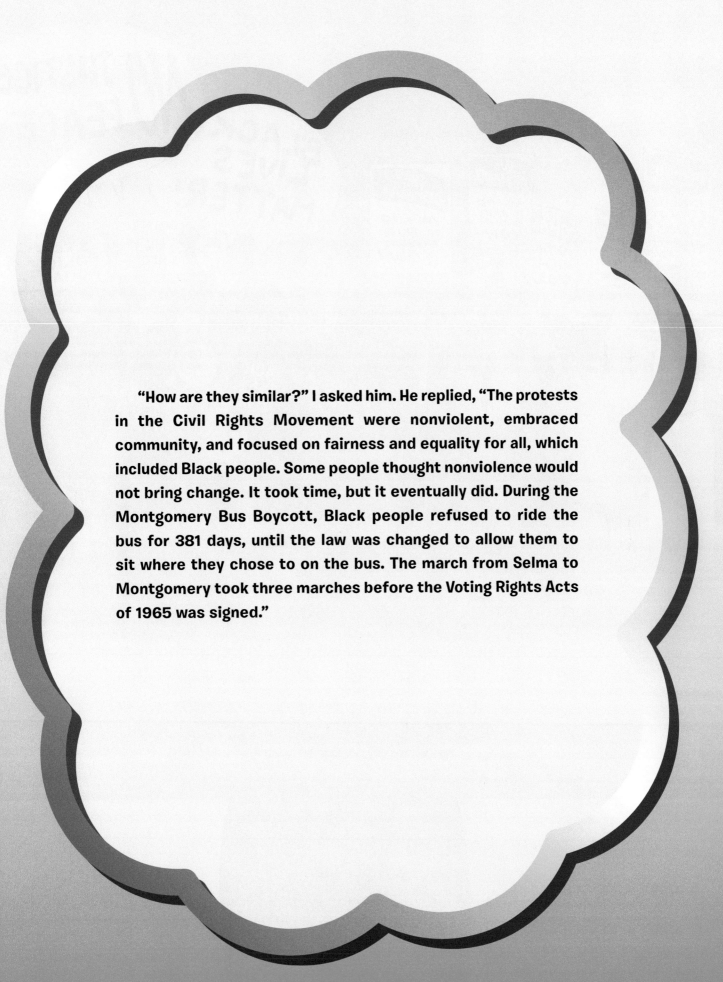

"How are they similar?" I asked him. He replied, "The protests in the Civil Rights Movement were nonviolent, embraced community, and focused on fairness and equality for all, which included Black people. Some people thought nonviolence would not bring change. It took time, but it eventually did. During the Montgomery Bus Boycott, Black people refused to ride the bus for 381 days, until the law was changed to allow them to sit where they chose to on the bus. The march from Selma to Montgomery took three marches before the Voting Rights Acts of 1965 was signed."

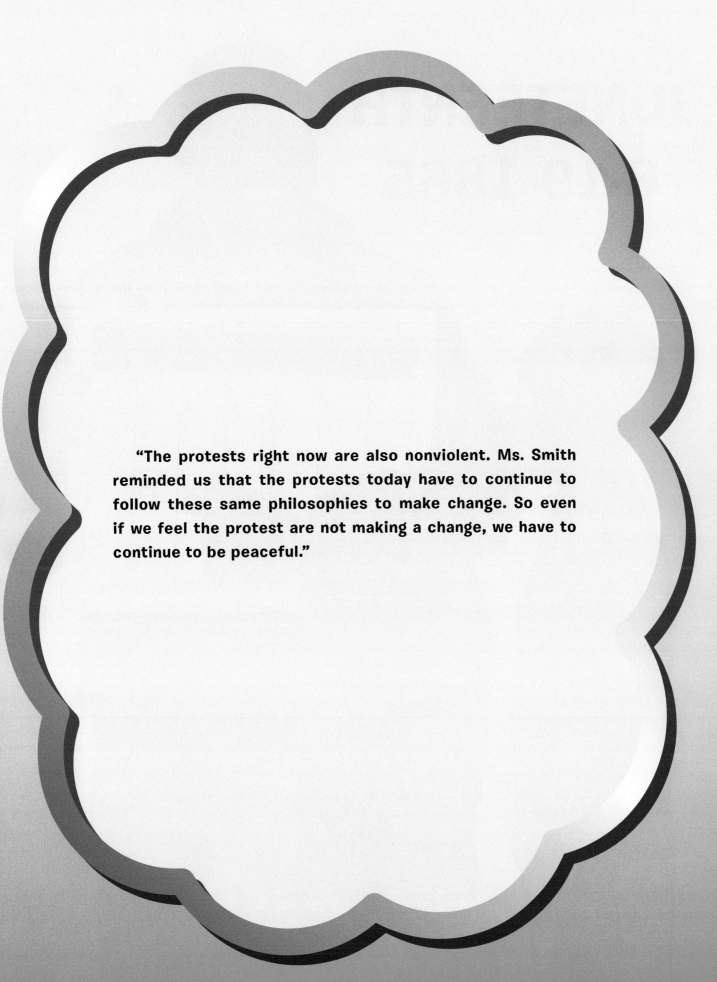

"The protests right now are also nonviolent. Ms. Smith reminded us that the protests today have to continue to follow these same philosophies to make change. So even if we feel the protest are not making a change, we have to continue to be peaceful."

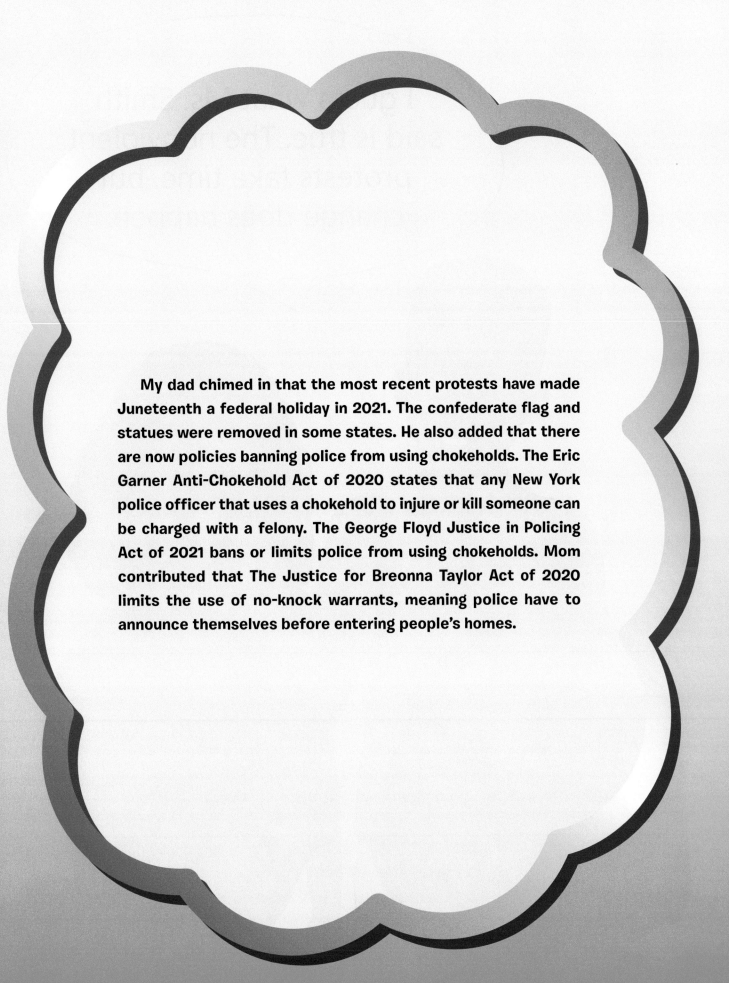

My dad chimed in that the most recent protests have made Juneteenth a federal holiday in 2021. The confederate flag and statues were removed in some states. He also added that there are now policies banning police from using chokeholds. The Eric Garner Anti-Chokehold Act of 2020 states that any New York police officer that uses a chokehold to injure or kill someone can be charged with a felony. The George Floyd Justice in Policing Act of 2021 bans or limits police from using chokeholds. Mom contributed that The Justice for Breonna Taylor Act of 2020 limits the use of no-knock warrants, meaning police have to announce themselves before entering people's homes.

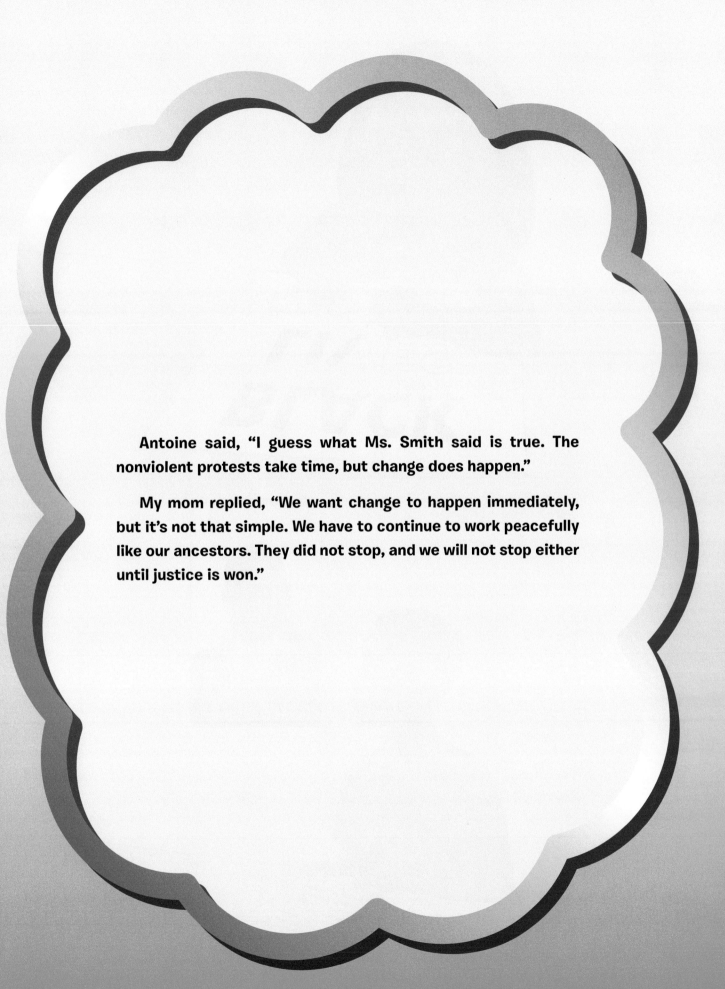

Antoine said, "I guess what Ms. Smith said is true. The nonviolent protests take time, but change does happen."

My mom replied, "We want change to happen immediately, but it's not that simple. We have to continue to work peacefully like our ancestors. They did not stop, and we will not stop either until justice is won."

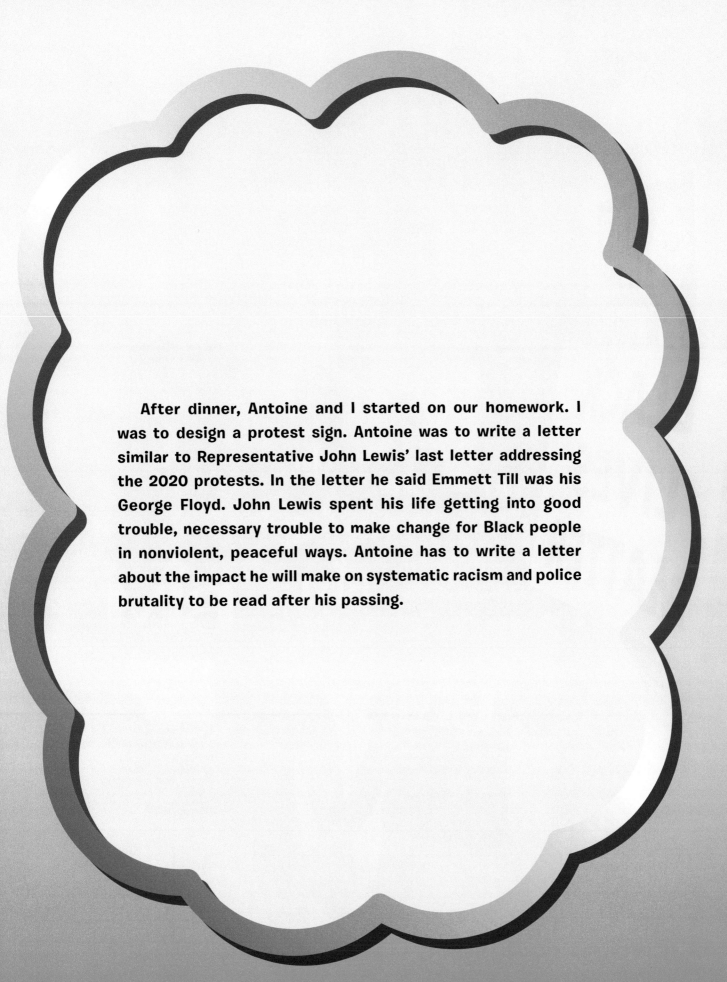

After dinner, Antoine and I started on our homework. I was to design a protest sign. Antoine was to write a letter similar to Representative John Lewis' last letter addressing the 2020 protests. In the letter he said Emmett Till was his George Floyd. John Lewis spent his life getting into good trouble, necessary trouble to make change for Black people in nonviolent, peaceful ways. Antoine has to write a letter about the impact he will make on systematic racism and police brutality to be read after his passing.

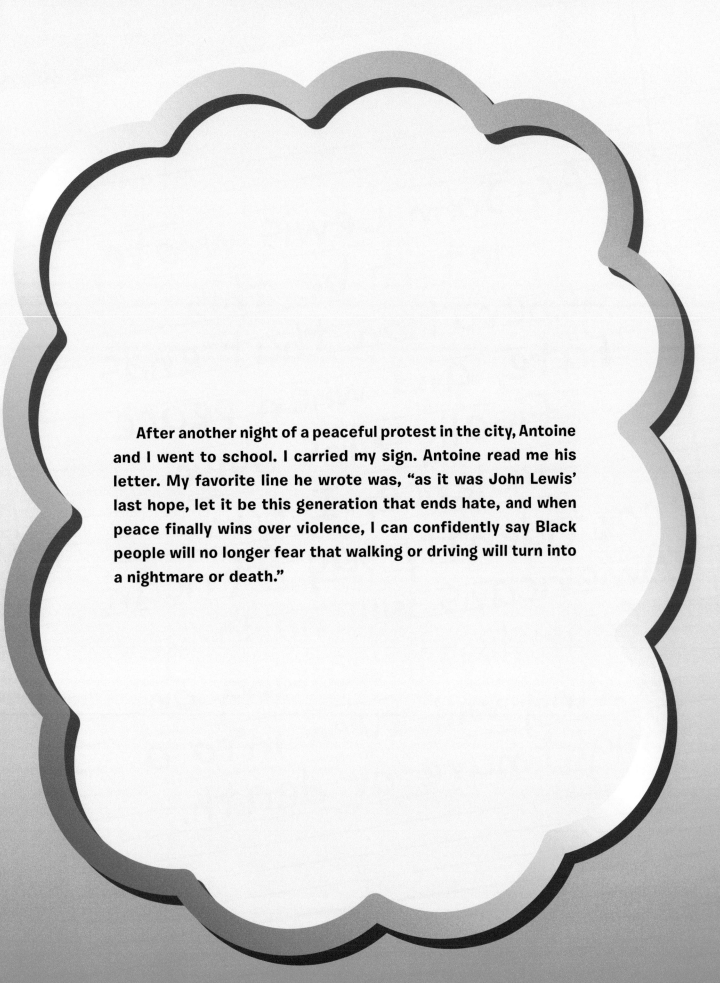

After another night of a peaceful protest in the city, Antoine and I went to school. I carried my sign. Antoine read me his letter. My favorite line he wrote was, "as it was John Lewis' last hope, let it be this generation that ends hate, and when peace finally wins over violence, I can confidently say Black people will no longer fear that walking or driving will turn into a nightmare or death."

As John Lewis wrote, let it be this generation that ends hate, and when peace finally wins over violence, I can confidently say African Americans will no longer fear that walking or driving will turn into a nightmare or death.

Printed in the United States
by Baker & Taylor Publisher Services